Hou s
Survive

by Emma Rattenbury

SCHOOL PUBLISHERS

Cover ©Photolibrary.com; 2 (c) ©Getty Images; 2 (b) ©Michael Turco Photography; 2 (t) ©Oxygen Group Photography/David M. Barron; 3 ©Getty Images; 4 ©Michael Turco Photography; 5 ©Photolibrary.com/Alamy; 6 ©Oxygen Group Photography/David M. Barron; 7 ©Photolibrary.com; 8 ©Getty Images.

Printed in China

ISBN 10: 0-15-351346-2
ISBN 13: 978-0-15-351346-6

Ordering Options
ISBN 10: 0-15-351211-3 (Grade 1 Advanced Collection)
ISBN 13: 978-0-15-351211-7 (Grade 1 Advanced Collection)
ISBN 10: 0-15-358038-0 (package of 5)
ISBN 13: 978-0-15-358038-3 (package of 5)

4 5 6 7 8 9 10 0940 15 14 13 12 11 10 09

All kinds of animals do things that help them survive.

Apes

This ape lives in the forest. It makes a nest. How does a nest help it to survive?

The nest is high in the trees. It keeps the ape warm and safe.

This one uses its fingers and toes to make a nest. It makes the nest from leaves and branches.

This ape has hair that is a red-brown color.

Toads

Toads look like frogs, but they are different. Toads only live on land. Many walk rather than hop.

This toad can puff itself up with air. How does puffing up help it survive?

Puffing up makes the toad look bigger than it is. This tricks an animal that may want to eat it. The toad looks too big to swallow.

This toad blends in with the rocks.

Harp Seals

Harp seals live where there is ice and snow. Baby seals have white fur. Each hair is clear like glass. The sun makes the fur look white. How does white fur help a seal survive?

The white fur helps the seal blend into the snow. Then it is hard to see. This keeps it safe from other animals that want to catch it.

The seal is swimming away. Good-bye, baby seal!